Knitted Owl Slippers With a Cuff

by

Janis Frank

Thank you for purchasing this book. This book remains the copyrighted property of the author, and may not be redistributed to others for commercial or non-commercial purposes. If you enjoyed this book, please encourage your friends to purchase their own copy from their favourite book retailer.

Thank you for your support and respecting the hard work of this author. The purchase of this book allows you to make and sell the physical items you create.

Table of Contents

Get ready to knit a pair of slippers that are as cozy as they are charming! This knitting pattern brings together the best of warmth and whimsy, featuring a delightful owl motif perched right on top of the foot. These adult-sized slippers have been crafted with both style and function in mind, thanks to a fitted cuff that hugs your ankle for extra warmth and coziness. Perfect for chilly mornings or relaxed evenings, these slippers will be a go-to pair for any owl lover.

This pattern is designed for knitters with a bit of experience—if you're comfortable with basic stitches, you'll be able to follow along with ease. And don't worry, you won't be left to navigate the trickier parts alone! I've included detailed, how-to videos to help guide you through each step, ensuring that even challenging sections feel doable. Before you know it, you'll have a cozy, owl-adorned pair of slippers that are sure to turn heads and keep feet warm.

From the soft cuff that wraps around your ankle to the intricate owl design on top, these slippers are truly a unique addition to any knitter's project list. So pick up your needles, gather your yarn, and get ready to create a little piece of woodland magic that's just for adults—your feet deserve it!

Things You Need

1 ball of worsted weight yarn (average 260 yard, 5 oz or 141 gram ball will be more than enough). You can use a second colour for the cuff.

2 sets of size 4 mm (US size 6) single point knitting needles.

Stitch holderi484

Cable Needle

Tapestry needle to sew in ends. You can also use this handy video tutorial to show you how to work in the ends while knitting these slippers, especially when changing colour from the cuff, sides and sole of the slipper. Take a photo of the QR code below with your phone or tablet. A link will pop up. Tap the link and the video on YouTube will start to play.

Gauge

With size 4 mm (US size 6) needles or *whatever size you need* to obtain the correct number of stitches and rows. Be sure to check your gauge otherwise the sizing won't be correct.

In *garter stitch*

2" = 9 sts

2" = 18 rows

Sizes (are written as such)

Women's 6-7 (**8-9,** 10-11, **12-13**)

Men's 5-6 (**7-8,** 9-10, **11-12**)

Cuff

With **CUFF** colour

Cast on 36 (38, 40, 42) loosely

✋**Row 1**: K across

Row 2: With the RIGHT side facing you, (K1 P2) across. Maintain this pattern with any remaining sts at the end of the row. ✋

Repeat from ✋ to ✋ 10 (**12**, 14, **16**) times *more* for a total of 12 (**14**, 16, **18**) rows

Next Row: With the **RIGHT** side facing, P across.

Next Row: K across. If cuff colour differs from the **MAIN** colour, break yarn now. Start the new colour when done knitting this row.

Next Row: K across for 13 (**15**, 17, **19**) rows. Break yarn.

Toe Flap

Next Row: With the **MAIN** colour and the **WRONG** side of the ribbing facing you, transfer the first 11 (12, 13, 14) stitches to a stitch holder. Reattach the yarn and ***knit the next 14 stitches*** (the start of the toe flap with the owl motif). Leave the remaining 11 (**12**, 13, **14**) stitches on the needle unworked.

How to use a st holder

The following rows are worked back and forth on the 14 toe flap stitches only!

Knit across for 7 (**9**, 9, **11**) rows.

Next Row (with the **RIGHT** side of the ribbing facing you): K3 P2 K4 P2 K3

Next Row (with the **WRONG** side of the ribbing facing you): K2 P1 K8 P1 K2

Next Row: K3 P8 K3

♦ **Next Row:** K2 P1 C4F C4B P1 K2

Take a photo with your phone or tablet of the QR codes to watch the videos showing how to make the cable sts. A link will pop up. Tap the link and the video will start.

How to C4F

How to C4B

Next Row: K3 P8 K3

♥ **Next Row:** K2 P1 K8 P1 K2

Next Row: K3 P8 K3 ♥ Repeat from ♥ to ♥ 2 more times

Next Row: Repeat row marked with ♦

Next Row: K3 P2 K4 P2 K3

♪ **Next Row:** K2 P1 K2 P4 K2 P1 K2

Next Row: K3 P2 K4 P2 K3 ♪ Repeat from ♪ to ♪ **3** more times

Next Row: Repeat row marked with ♦

Next Row: K across for 5 (**7**, 7, **9**) rows.

Sides of Foot

This is where you're going to need the extra set of knitting needles. You'll be knitting back and forth in rows but the turn around the toe is too tight to use circular needles. For this, you'll put the 14 toe flap stitches on one of your extra needles. It's a little unconventional, but it works.

Next Row: With the *RIGHT* side facing, transfer the 11 (12, 13, 14) stitches from the stitch holder onto one of your needles. Attach your yarn and knit the 11 (12, 13, 14) stitches. Pick up 21 (22, 23, 24) stitches evenly along the edge of the toe flap. (All of these stitches are on *ONE* needle. (32, 34, 36, 38) stitches on this needle)

With another needle, knit the 14 stitches of the toe flap. (14 stitches on this needle)

With another needle, pick up 21 (22, 23, 24) stitches evenly along the side of the toe flap. Knit the remaining 11 (12, 13, 14) stitches on the next needle. (32, 34, 36, 38) stitches on this needle)

You should now have 3 needles holding stitches with all the points pointing as shown below when laid flat. You also have one spare needle to knit with. You are now going to knit in rows, back and forth with these three needles. Once you finish knitting all the stitches on one needle, move on to the next needle (the point of the needle is right there) until you complete the row.

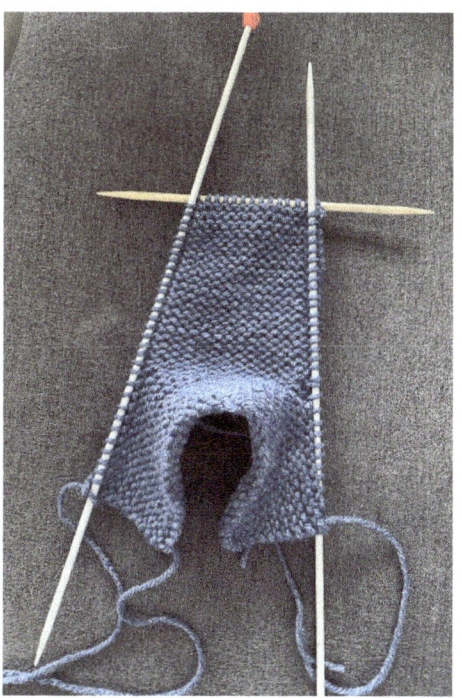

I used a double pointed needle to work my 14 stitches
for the toe only because it was handy. A regular needle works!

Knit the next 8 (**10,** 12, **14**) rows

There are 4 (**5,** 6, **7**) ridges on the tip of the toe.

The following photo shows the 5 ridges for the women's size 8-9 or the men's 7-8.

These are the ridges picked up along the side.

Next Row: With **WRONG** side facing. Cast off all the stitches from the first needle *loosely*. You'll need to pass the last stitch from the first needle over the first stitch of the toe flap stitches (second needle).

Using the same needle that now has one stitch, knit the remaining 13 stitches of the toe flap. Cast off all the stitches from the third needle *loosely*. Break yarn.

Making the Sole

If you need more help than the photos provide, you can watch the how-to video by taking a pic of the QR code below or by using this link - https://bit.ly/knit-the-sole Both the link and the QR code start the video in the correct section. No need to find the spot. I already have it cued up for you.

Next Row: With the **RIGHT** side facing, attach yarn and knit the first stitch of the cast off stitches by the toe flap (cast off stitch on the right by the point of the needle).

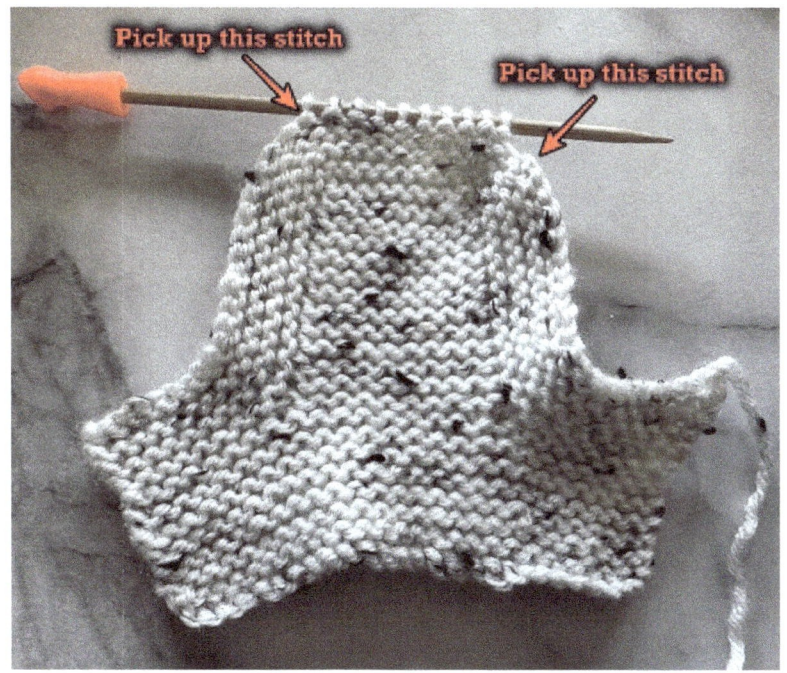

Pick up this stitch at the start of the row.

K2tog. Knit to the last 2 stitches K2tog. Pick up the cast off stitch by the point of your needle. (14 stitches).

Pick up this stitch at the end of the row.

Quick tip – wrap the yarn counterclockwise around your needle and turn it down to pull the yarn through the cast off stitch on the right. If you have a hard time doing this, you can also use a crochet hook to pull the loop through and place that loop on your working needle.

You now are working back and forth along the bottom of the foot picking up one cast off stitch on each side as you go.

Next Row: Knit across.

ʤ Next Row: Pick up the next stitch of the cast off stitches. K2tog. Knit to the last 2 stitches K2tog. Pick up the cast off stitch on the other side of the slipper by the point of your needle. (14 stitches).

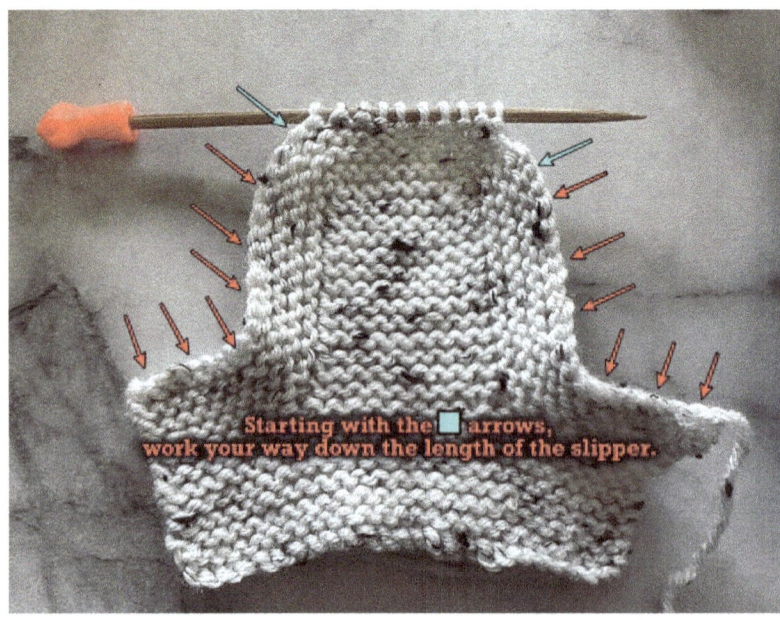

Next Row: Knit across ʤ

Repeat from ʤ to ʤ down the entire length of the foot. There are equal number of cast off stitches along each side. How many rows varies depending on the size of slipper you're making. Be sure to end with a completed knit across row.

Starting the sole. Right side.

Working your way down while making the sole. Wrong side.

Continuing to work down the length of the sole

Still further down the sole. Note how the cast off edges are being picked up as you go.
Keep working your way down the length of the sole until you've picked up all the cast off stitches.

Making the Heel

If you need more help than the photos provide, you can watch the how-to video by taking a pic of the QR code below or by using this link – https://bit.ly/knit-the-heel.Both the link and the QR code start the video in the correct section. No need to find the spot. I already have it cued up for you.

You're now going to make a small triangle to fit in the back of the heel. You're going to fill this space in the slipper.

Next Row: With the **RIGHT** side facing, pick up a stitch in the row closest to the sole of the slipper. Count how many ridges it is for the size you are making. K2tog twice. Knit to the last 4 stitches. K2tog twice. Count down the same number of ridges on the other side and pick up a stitch in the space beneath it. (12 stitches).

The photo above shows 9 rows of ridges.
These are rows you knit to form the edges of the slipper.

Stitch picked up on the right edge in the 9th row shown above

After you K2tog at the end of the row, you'll pick up a stitch here.

Stitch picked up at the end of the row.

Next Row: Knit across.

Next Row: Count down one ridge less than the previous row and pick up a stitch in the space beneath it. K2tog. Knit until the last 2 stitches. K2tog. Count down the same number of ridges and pick up a stitch in the space beneath it on the other side.

Next Row: Knit across. ⓠ Repeat from ⓠ to ⓠ until 6 stitches remain.

Next Row: Pick up a stitch beneath the next ridge. K2tog 3 times. Pick up a stitch in the space beneath the next ridge on the other side.

Next Row: Knit across.

Next Row: K2tog, K1, K2tog. Pass the middle stitch on your working needle over the stitch on the left. Pass the stitch on the right over the stitch on the left. (Or you can turn your work and K3tog).

Break yarn leaving a length of yarn long enough (8ish inches) to sew up the remaining seam.

Make another slipper.

Yes, they do look a little boxy when they're done and not on a foot. The stretch of the garter stitch allows these slippers to stretch around the contours of any foot easily.

Hints and Tips

If you want a longer cuff at the top, work more rows than stated at the beginning when you cast on. Make sure to increase the same amount of garter stitch rows and ribbed rows equally. If increasing 10 rows, do so on both.

When picking up stitches from the cast off row, be sure you're really moving on to the next cast off stitch! It's an easy mistake to pick up a stitch in a stitch you already picked up. If in doubt, give the needle holding the stitches a bit of a tug. You'll see the yarn move slightly at the very back, closest to the needle. Pick up a stitch at the NEXT cast off stitch.

If you don't have the same number of stitches on both sides when you are forming the sole, you may have picked up a stitch twice in one stitch or missed one. Don't worry! This is fixable. You can skip one cast off stitch if you need to make it even, or pick up a cast off stitch twice on the other side. There's enough stretch in the slipper that any puckering this causes won't be overly visible if you're off by a stitch or two.

To speed up finishing the slippers and not have so many ends to sew in, hold the yarn ends to the back of your work as you knit. You can watch the how to video here - how to work in the ends while knitting these slippers. You can also scan the QR code below.

Abbreviations

K – knit

P - purl

K2tog – knit 2 together

K3tog – knit 3 together

Side note: I use both versions of the terminology when it comes to cable stitches. I've been corrected that I'm using the wrong one for both occasions so it's a no win for me. What I mean is that C4F is the same technique as C2F. Just like how C2B is the same as C4B. Do you think of it as the just the stitches you're pulling or the number of stitches you're using in total when you do it? It's a personal choice, I guess.

C4F - Pick up the next 2 stitches with your cable needle. Pull the stitches to the FRONT of your work. Knit the next 2 stitches on your non-working needle. Knit the 2 stitches from the cable needle. Watch this video to see how. How to C4F or Cable 4 Forward.

C4B - Pick up the next 2 stitches with your cable needle. Pull the stitches to the BACK of your work. Knit the next 2 stitches on your non-working needle. Knit the 2 stitches from the cable needle. Watch this video to see how. How to C4B or Cable 4 Back

st – stitch

sts - stitches

Like all of my patterns you have my permission to sell and/or give away the slippers that you make using this pattern. You are NOT permitted to reprint this pattern in any form unless you have obtained my written permission to do so.

If you have any questions, please feel free to leave a comment or send me your questions at kweenbee_crafts@hotmail.ca.

Help Support My Work!

Follow me on Instagram, Facebook, Pinterest and YouTube. Every follow, subscribe, thumbs up, like, heart and share help increase my popularity on the web and get more viewers to my work. It costs you nothing but helps me sooooo much!

If you would like to help a little more, you can always become a Website Member to download and print over 30 patterns. Or you can support me by becoming a Patron on Patreon or you can make a single time donation at Buy Me a Coffee.

You can use any of these QR codes to find out more.

Website Member **Patreon** **Buy Me a Coffee**

More FREE knitting patterns on my website

I'm always creating new patterns and I post every one of them over on my website. It is an ever growing list so you might want to check out my page at **KweenBee.com**. I design new patterns as I get time. I aim to add a couple new ones each month so the list is always growing!

Below is a VERY small example of the other patterns that I have on the website. There are over 50 patterns that are free to read online. Make sure to check it out! I'm always writing and designing new patterns!

Knitted Deer Slippers

Cozy Lace Up Slippers for Adults

Owl Bucket Hat

Winter Beanie Toque or Touque or Tuque with Vertical Stripes

Ultra Thick Slip-On Bootie Slippers

How to Knit a Beanie Hat – with OWLS!

Minimalist Round Toe Slippers

Texting Mittens

To make it even easier, you can take a photo of the QR code below with your phone or tablet. A link will pop up. Tap that link and it will take you right to the webpage to see all of the patterns including those above.

You can also do a search for the titles online if QR codes are something that you feel you are unable or don't want to use it.

When you are on your favourite search engine like Google, Bing, Yahoo, etc. Enter the term *Kweenbee* and the title as it is written below (capitalization isn't important). It will pop up for you in the search results and be super-easy to find.

For example, enter it like this:

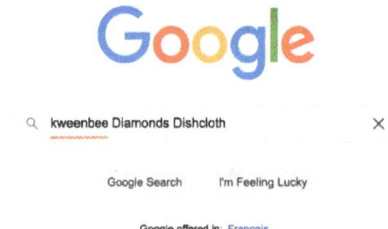

Your results will have my pattern at the very top...usually. Depending on the popularity of the pattern, you may get a link to Pinterest or Ravelry first. Don't worry! All of those options have links back to my original patterns, too!

Follow Me on Social Media

Take a photo with your phone or tablet of the QR codes below. A link will appear. Click the link to go straight to my social media page.